Google Drive And Docs

In 1 Hour

Beginners Guide to Mastering Google Drive and Docs with Illustrations

DERRICK

RICHARD

Copyright

Table of Contents

Chapter 3

Chapter 1

Getting Started With Google Apps

Google does not require any form of introduction. It is the biggest search engine in the world, but it doesn't end there. They provide several services that enhance productivity and share information among google users. This brings us to the question, what are google apps? Google apps are a suite of platform-independent productivity applications. What this means is that they can be accessed on just about any device, platforms, or operating system (Windows, Mac, mobile devices, android, iOS, etc.), allowing users to synchronize and integrate the services provided by these apps seamlessly. This means emails, calendars, contacts, files, and many more can be shared among different users in a collaborative environment.

Some useful Google apps will be briefly discussing in this chapter. For instance, Gmail, Google Drive, Google Docs, Sheets, Forms, Slides, Drawings, and Google Site. Others include Google Collaboration, Keeps, Calendar, Photos, Contacts, etc. We will also look at comprehensive keyboard shortcuts for Google Drive and Docs.

Gmail

Some years ago, Google created its email client called Gmail, which has become one of the top providers of email services around the world today. It comes with a standard address that ends in @gmail.com and integrates contact that synchronizes with your email. Google also provides a corporate version that ends with your domain name. Gmail became so popular and was used by individuals, institutions, and businesses to send emails. It is also a fast and friendly email service that is also secure and prevents spam. However, a Gmail account provides more than just email services; it allows access to a wide variety of Google apps and services. This means you need a Gmail account to access a range of Google Services and Apps.

Google Drive

This is one of the apps you have access to when you have a Gmail account. Google Drive is a cloud storage and file backup system which provides you with 15GB of disk space to host all kinds of files, photos, videos, etc. for free. Although 15GB is a lot of space to get for free, however, if you need more storage space, you can always buy from Google. Within Google Drive, you can create all kinds of documents with Google's web-based office suite. The suite has Docs, Sheets, Slides, Forms etc; and files created with these suites are easily converted to any standard file format.

Google Docs

Google Docs is a simple but powerful word processor, just like Microsoft Word. You can type text documents and use Google search within Docs for whatever topic you are working on without leaving your document. Anyone with the right privileges can also access, share and collaborate on a Google Doc files.

Google Sheets

Still, within Google Drive, we have the Google spreadsheets. This is a handy spreadsheet program for organizing data and work with tonnes of formulas for calculations and data analysis as you would in Microsoft Excel.

Google Slides

This is another Google suites service used for creating stunning presentations like Microsoft Powerpoints.

Google Forms

Another vital Google Suite app is Google Forms. With Google Forms, you can create forms with different types of questions to take surveys or gather data/feedbacks from friends, customers, students, etc. The submitted data can then be analyzed in an associated spreadsheet in Google Sheets linked to the form.

Google Calendar

This app is like every other calendar app, with all the regular calendar features. You can change your views to daily, weekly and monthly views. Google Calendar is a useful app in which meetings, lectures, or events can be organized. With Google Calendar, you never forget an appointment. It is used for establishing notifications and inviting your contacts to a scheduled event. Because Google Apps are collaborative, Google calendars can be shared in public or private and can also be published to web sites. The schedules can be viewed in different colors with the ability to overlay things like Holidays on birthdays on Google Map.

Google Groups

Google groups allow users to create groups from their contacts and use them as mailing lists, or as a base for sharing documents.

Google Sites

Google Site is an app that provides a fast and straightforward way to create sophisticated web pages with the aid of inbuilt Google templates.

Blogger

With Blogger, you can build your blogs on topics of your interest either by yourself or in collaboration with others.

Google Classroom

If you are a teacher and your educational institution uses Google apps, you can take advantage of Google Classroom. It is a friendly e-learning site where teachers can interact with their students, give assignments, mark assignments, and create interactive content.

Google Plus

Google Plus is a social media platform like Facebook. It allows users to create a public profile and syncs photos for easy upload. Google Plus also provides automatic backup for mobile photos to its cloud system. Each app in Google suite has an associated social network profile in Google Plus.

YouTube

Youtube is one of Google's apps which allow users to create their own video channel and upload their recordings. Most of these channels can be monetized.

Google Maps

The Google Maps app, also referred to as Google navigation, is a mobile app that provides an efficient GPS service to get driving directions in cities. Users can also carry out activities such as looking up local businesses, searching for addresses, view traffic situations when they commute with the aid of Google Maps. With Google Maps, users can identify and also navigate their way through to locations where their contacts reside.

Google Voice

Google voice, which runs on iOS, Android, and web, gives you a private phone number that can ring to five other mobile or traditional phones. It can also call any other conventional phone except another Google Voice number. Google Voice allows you to make and receive calls, allowing you to retain privacy to your cell phones and office phones. This app also provides you with a web-based app for managing voice mail and text messages.

Google Hangout

Google Hangout is similar to Skype with audio and video call capability between computers and mobile devices, including group calls. It is ideal for communicating with friends, students, or customers in real-time. You can also call a landline from your computer with Google Hangouts. This app is touted to replace the Google Voice app in the future.

Google Apps for Education

If you are a teacher, note that in addition to the private Google accounts, there is also a free version of Google Apps for Education that any academic institution can easily request, using their internet domain name. Also, note that there are no specific numbers of users (students and teachers) on this app. The administrator(s) can create as many user accounts as they wish for all their students and teachers.

Accessing Google Apps

There are several ways to access Google apps. The easiest way, however, is to open your Gmail account > click on the app's icon on the top-right corner of the screen.

Here you will find all the google apps and their icons. In the next chapter, we will go into Google Drive and Docs in detail.

Chapter 2

Google Drive

Account Setup

In this section, we will look at the basics of Google drive and how to get the most out of it. Before you can have access to google apps, you need to sign up for a Gmail account if you don't have one. To do this, visit www.gmail.com > Click on create account

Google

Sign in

to continue to Gmail

Email or phone

Forgot email?

Not your computer? Use Guest mode to sign in privately. Learn more

Create account   Next

English (United States) ▼   Help   Privacy   Terms

Indicate if you wish to open a personal account by click on 'For myself' or a business account by clicking on 'to manage my business.

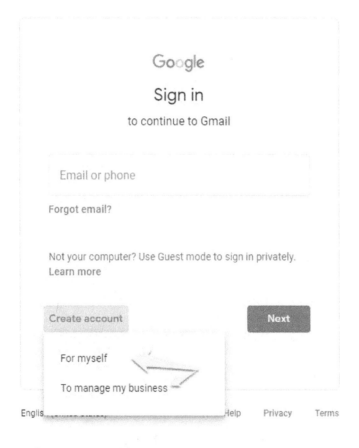

Next, fill-up the form, with your names, your Gmail address, for instance, derrickrichard@ gmail.com, then create a password and

confirm the password. > Click next. On the
next window, enter your phone number.

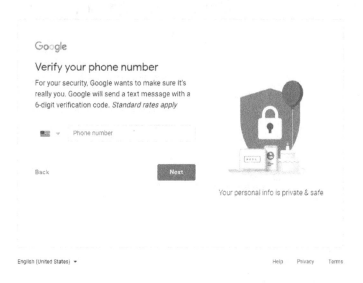

A verification code will be sent to the number.

Enter the verification code in the box provided and click "Verify." If you wish to receive a voice message with the verification code, click on "Call instead." With your phone number verified, you can now log into your Gmail account.

There are a couple of ways to access Google drive, as we mentioned in the previous chapter. While Logged in to your Gmail account, click on the Google App icon at the upper left corner.

Next, click on "Drive." This will take you to the Google Drive Home Page.

Alternatively, type in the URL address – drive.google.com.

Creating folders, Docs, and sheet

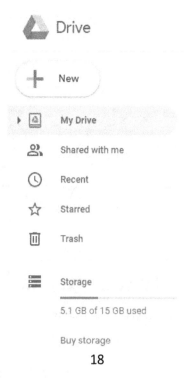

When you access Google drive for the first time, you have access to a handy PDF document that Google provides to give you an excellent overview of how to use the Drive. On the left of the Google drive home screen are menus – New, My Drive, Shared with me, Google Photos, Recent, Starred, Trash, and Upgrade Storage. At the lower left is a menu to 'Get Drive for Mac' if you use Mac. Now let's look at the menu items one after the other to understand how they function.

New

Clicking on 'New' gives us a lot of menu options. They include folder, File upload, and folder upload.

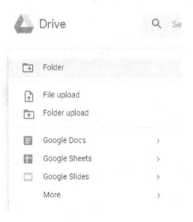

Other menu items under 'New' include Google Docs, Sheets, Slides, and more.

Creating A New Folder

You can create new storage folders to help you organize content on your drive by Clicking on the 'Folder' menu.

This opens up a 'New Folder' dialogue box with a default name 'Untiled folder.' Rename the new folder and click on the 'Create' button.

Uploading Files and Folders

Just below the 'folder' menu is the 'File Upload.' The file upload allows a user to upload an existing file (e.g., photos, documents, videos, audio, etc.) from their device e.g., PC or mobile device to their Google drive. To do this, click on 'File Upload' > then search within your PC or mobile device storage to locate the file you wish to upload to your Google Drive Cloud Storage and click on it. Next, click 'Open,' and this kick-starts the upload process. On the other hand, you can upload an entire folder on your device to your Google drive. Click on 'Folder upload' > search for the folder you wish to upload and click on it > Next, click on 'Upload.' A warning message pops up to confirm you trust the source of the folder, and you click 'Upload' to confirm.

Opening Google Docs From Google Drive

We can access Google Docs from the 'New' menu. Click on 'New,' and when the 'New' Menu opens up, click on 'Google Docs.'

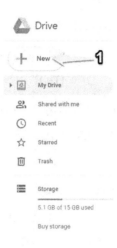

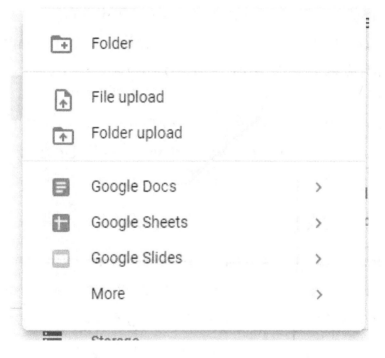

This opens the Docs on a separate tab. If you click on the arrow by the Google Docs menu, you have the option to choose between a 'Blank Document' or from several pre-installed Doc templates.

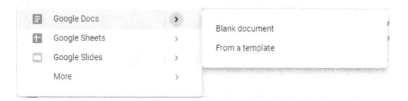

Click on 'blank documents' to open up a blank document.

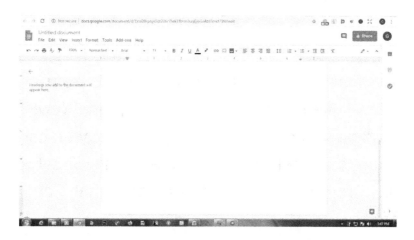

On the other hand, clicking on the 'from a template' option opens up a variety of templates from a template gallery that users can pick from.

We will look at Google Docs in detail in the next chapter.

Opening Google Sheet From Google Drive

We can also access Google Sheet from the "New" Menu by Simply clicking on 'New' > 'Google Sheets.' Like Google docs, you have options to select between a blank Sheet or pick from the variety of templates that Google offers.

We will dive into Google Sheets in detail in the Book "Google Drive and Spreadsheet" by Derrick Richard.

Opening Google Slides From Google Drive

Like the Google Docs and Sheets, Google Slide can equally be accessed through the 'New' Menu. Click on 'New' > 'Google Slides', and a new Google Slides Window will be opened on a new tab. We could also select between the blank Google Slide worksheet the variety of templates.

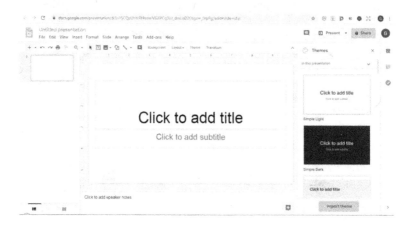

Opening other Apps through Google Drive

We could access other Google apps like Google forms, drawings, Maps, Sites, App

Script, and Jamboard via the 'New' Menu by merely clicking on 'New' > 'More.' Here we select any of the apps we want.

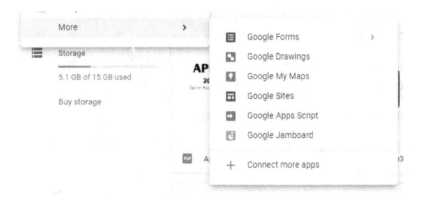

We could also link other apps from the Google Suite Marketplace to Google Drive by clicking on 'Connect More Apps' and selecting from a range of Google Suites.

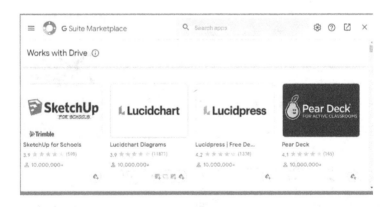

Sharing, Tagging and Collaborating

Collaboration is a vital feature when it comes to using Google Drive because one of the essential elements of google drive is the ability to communicate and share information with other people. Let's say we have created a folder on Google Drive and have uploaded a variety of documents in this folder that needs to be seen or edited by a colleague or collaborators, and we need to give them access to this folder on our drive. What you do is select the folder or document by single-clicking on it > then click on the little avatar of the person with the plus sign at the top right.

This brings up a dialogue box in which you can add the email addresses of those you wish to share your file, document, or folder.

You can also add a note of what you want them to do with the file or documents in the folder. Now, you will be able to share the folder or grant collaborator(s) access to the folder.

Next, you can grant the collaborator(s) permission to be able to either organize, add information, and edit the files or document(s). Collaborators can also be given view-only access to the document or file without being able to edit it.

Click 'Done' and 'Send' when you are through with adding your collaborators and granting them necessary permissions. They get an e-mail inviting them to collaborate on the folder or file sent to them. Alternatively, you can share documents or files with your collaborators with the steps below:

- Click on the file or folder you wish to share
- Click on the share averter ☌⁺
- Click on 'Get Shareable link.'

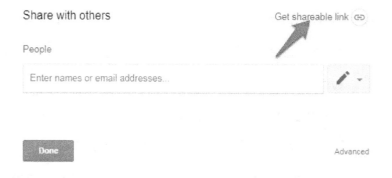

It generates a link you can share with your collaborators.

- Click on 'Copy link'

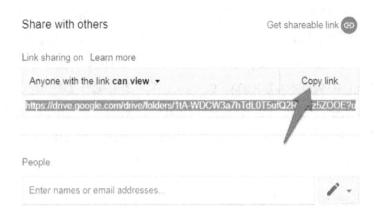

Share with others   Get shareable link

Link sharing on   Learn more

Anyone with the link can view ▾   Copy link

https://drive.google.com/drive/folders/1tA-WDCW3a7hTdL0T5ufQ2H...z5ZOOE?u

People

Enter names or email addresses...

Done   Advanced

- With this, whoever gets the link, can only view the document or file. They won't be able to edit or comment because the default permission is "Anyone with the link can view."
- If you wish to grant them more permission, click on the drop-down arrow by the default permission to access a variety of rights, you can explore.

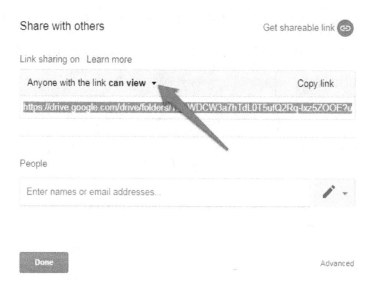

- Now, select from the list. Click on more to access additional link sharing options.

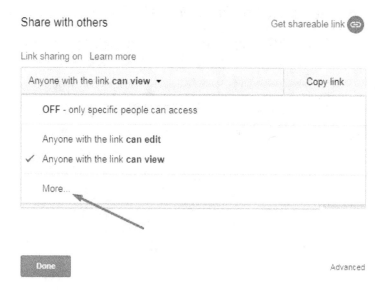

- Here, you can determine how collaborators can use the document or folder link you shared.

- You get additional sharing options when you click "advanced" at the bottom right of the "Share with Others" dialogue box.

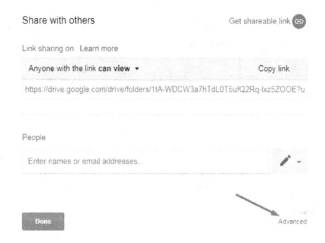

- The Advanced feature is one of the most important features you will be using as you get used to collaborating in Google Drive.

- The advance sharing features give you additional sharing options for your document or file link you generated. The features are the same if you are sharing a document, spreadsheet, or folders with different documents. With the advanced settings, a folder with various documents can be assigned different permissions for each document within the folder with your collaborator(s).

Sharing and Collaborating Within Google Docs

We can edit and collaborate within Google Docs using different modes. We can also leave and respond to comments as well as tag collaborators in those comments. Below is a Google Doc with text. This document can be shared with a collaborator to get their feedback and also edit.

To do this, click on the "Share" button at the top right corner and follow the steps for sharing document links and collaborating.

You can also comment on aspects of the contents you want looked at, or edited by collaborators. For instance, I have a question on a section in my blog post, and I want my collaborator to look at it. What I will do is highlight that section > when I do that, the comment icon pops up.

Next, click on it to open the comment box.

You can then leave a comment for your collaborator and click on "Comment" to send it across. The collaborator gets a notification with the highlighted section and effects whatever change you want or respond to the question you asked in the comment section. When the issues are sorted out, you or the collaborator clicks on "Resolve" to remove the comment(s).

; 10 Operating System can be installed on a MacOS with the aid of
called Bootcamp. Before you get started, ensure your Mac is
)le with the newest version of the Bootcamp installation process.
check this by clicking the Apple logo in the upper-left corner of the
ind click on "about this Mac". As long as you have a 2015 mac (or
a 2013 mac pro (or later), you are good to go with the installation
If you have a Mac older than those years, you will still be able to
'indows Bootcamp, but your process may look a little bit different
steps outlined in this book. To get started, you need a legitimate
Windows 10 and ISO format for this installation. This can be
ed and downloaded directly from Microsoft website. If you choose
load from the Microsoft web page, ensure you select the April

Tagging a Collaborator

We use the plus "+" sign to tag a collaborator to work on documents. For instance, let's say you are collaborating on a document with several of your staff, and they all have editing permissions, but you have an issue you want a collaborator to act on, you can tag that collaborator to resolve the specified problem. For instance, Roy is my staff and a collaborator, and I want him to respond to a section of a file, instead of just typing in the comment "Roy, can you work on this a bit more?" I will tag him using the plus sign, and it will look like this +Roy@gmail.com, can you work on this a bit more? > then hit the reply button.

compatible with the newest version of the Bootcamp installation process. You can check this by clicking the Apple logo in the upper-left corner of the screen and click on "about this Mac". As long as you have a 2015 mac (or later) or a 2013 mac pro (or later), you are good to go with the installation process. If you have a Mac older than those years, you will still be able to install Windows Bootcamp, but your process may look a little bit different from the steps outlined in this book. To get started, you need a legitimate copy of Windows 10 and ISO format for this installation. This can be purchased and downloaded directly from Microsoft website. If you choose to download from the Microsoft web page, ensure you select the April version as the October version is not compatible with this Bootcamp installation process – also select your language – select "64-bit download"

With this, Roy gets a notification that he has been tagged. He logs in and makes suggestions based on the comment(s).

Google Docs, as we stated earlier, is very collaborative and can be used in three separate modes for collaboration. The first one is editing mode. This allows collaborators to edit a shared document without any form of restrictions, a collaborator clicks on the 'mode' icon at the top left and select "Edit." This allows them to edit the text in the shared document.

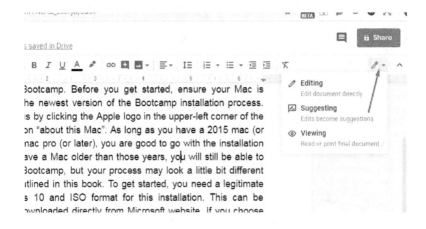

Collaborator(s) can make suggestions on specific aspects of the document if the "Suggesting mode" is selected. This is great when you are proofreading for others. This suggestion(s) can either be accepted or rejected. In Suggesting mode, suggestions are underlined by a green line, and a comment box pops up by the side. You can grant Collaborators suggesting rights by clicking on the 'mode' icon > select "Suggesting."

later) or a 2013 mac pro (or later), you are good to go with the installation process. If you have a Mac older than those years, you will still be able to install Windows Bootcamp, but your process may look a little bit different from the steps outlined in this book. To get started, you need a legitimate copy of Windows 10 and ISO format for this installation. This can be purchased and downloaded directly from Microsoft website. If you choose to download from the Microsoft web page, ensure you select the April version as the October version is not compatible with this Bootcamp installation process – also select your language – select "64-bit download" and download should start automatically. I think we should add more information to this blog post

Collaborator's suggestions are accepted by clicking on the checkmark or rejected by clicking the 'X'.

When the checkmark is clicked, the green suggestion line goes off, and the highlighted part becomes part of the text. When this is completed, you can then switch back to editing mode.

The third mode is the "View Only Mode" – here, collaborators can only view the file without the ability to edit or comment (make suggestions).

Deleting Items From Drive

It is very easy to delete files or folders from your Google Drive. If you are using a PC, Left-click on the file or folder you wish to delete and drag it across to the 'trash' on the right corner of the window.

Alternatively, you can delete a file or folder from your Google Drive account by right-clicking on the item, then scroll down and click on "Remove."

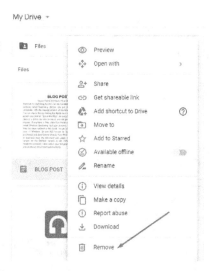

A third way to delete an item from the drive is – single-click on the item to highlight it, then click on the trash can icon at the top-right.

Deleted items or folders can be restored from the Trash. To do this, click on the trash icon, single-click on the item you wish to restore >

Click on the "restore from trash" icon, and your file or folder is restored to the Drive.

You can choose to delete an item forever to free up more disk space by clicking on the "Delete forever" icon.

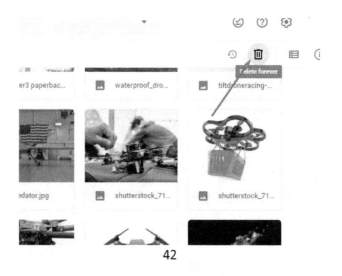

You can organize folders and files within Google Drive by either moving them around, rename them, view their details, make a duplicate copy or download them into a mobile device or PC. To do this, single-click on the item (file or folder), > then click of the ellipsis at the top-right of the dashboard.

With this, you can open the file with the Google App ideal for it, add a shortcut to the item, move it to another folder, rename it, view details of the file, make a duplicate copy or download it from cloud to your device. You can also move a file(s) into a folder by simply dragging them into the folder.

Shared With Me

The shared with me menu is where you find files, folders, videos, audios, and documents others shared with you for collaboration.

Files can be moved from the "Shared with Me" folder, into other folders within Google Drive. To do this, drag the file towards "My Drive." A drop-down menu opens up, showing all the folders on your Drive. You can then drop the file in any of the folders you prefer.

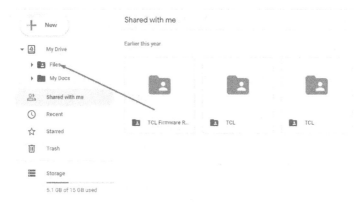

Color Code Folders

Color coding a folder is an accessibility feature for those that are visually impaired. To color-code a folder, select the folder > click on the three dots at the top right of the Google drive dashboard > scroll down and click on "Change color."

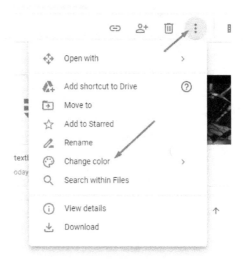

45

From the color pane, select any color for the selected folder.

The color of folder is then changed to the selected color.

Chapter 3

Google Docs

In the previous chapter, we looked at Google Drive and some aspects of Google Docs. In this chapter, we will look at Google Docs in detail.

Creating Docs Files

To create a Google Docs file, log into your Google Drive Account. In the URL, type drive.google.com > click on 'New' on the top left corner > scroll down to Google Docs. You may choose to open a blank document or select from a range of templates. Alternatively, you can type 'docs.new' in the URL of a Google chrome browser.

Give Your File a Name

The new document is given a default file name "Untitled document" which is displayed at the top left of the docs interface.

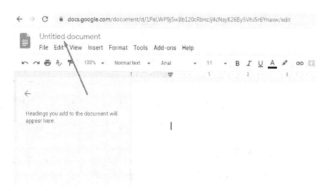

The first step after opening a new Docs file is to give it a title. Change the default title to something easier to find on the Drive. Click on 'File' > 'Rename.'

In this illustration, we will rename the doc file as 'DEMO.' A star and a folder icon pop up after renaming the file title.

The star icon allows users to search for their documents on Google Drive quickly while the folder icon enables users to select a desti- nation folder for the new file. Click on the folder icon and select a destination folder where your document or file is to be saved. Once you choose a destination folder, click on "Move."

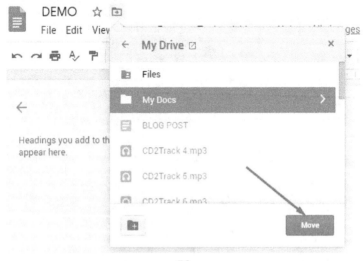

If there is no preexisting folder(s) on your drive, click on the folder with a plus sign to create a new folder.

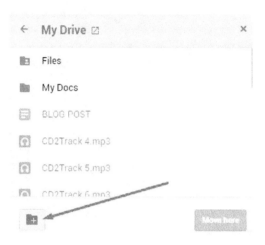

Next, give the new folder a name – for instance, we will use "My Folder" as the name of our new folder in this illustration. Then click on the "Create Folder" checkmark.

Create a new folder in My Drive

Finally, Click on "Move here" and your newly created docs file will be moved to the New folder.

The Docs Interface

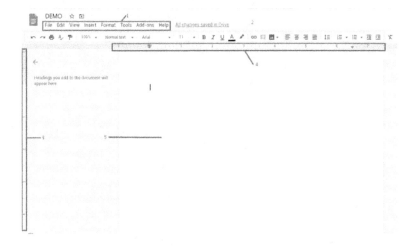

1 – Menu Bar

2 – Tool Bar

3 – Vertical ruler

4- Horizontal ruler

5 – Work Space

At the top of the Google docs interface, is the menu bar. Here we have the File, Edit, View, Insert, Format, Tools, Add-ons, and the Help menu. Below the Menu bar is the tools bar.

The tools bar hold different file editing icons. Below the Tools bar is the Horizontal ruler. The horizontal ruler allows users to adjust margins and also change indentation on the document. You can turn them ON or remove them. To remove the ruler, click on "View" > "Show ruler." This action eliminates the checkmark next to "Show ruler." The rulers can be made to reappear again on the docs interface by clicking on "View" > "Show ruler," and the checkmark appears.

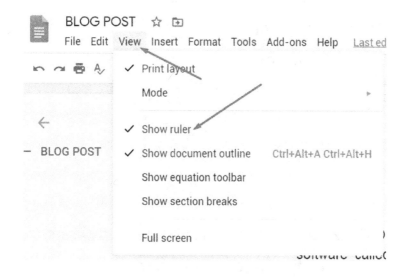

Formating the Text

As with every word processor, you can format text after typing. We will look at some formating options, one after the other, in this section.

Font Style

Arial   ▼

Several font styles come with Google Docs, and you can choose any that suits the job at hand. To change the font style of your text,

- Highlight the entire text or a section your wish to change by pressing and holding the left button on your mouse, then drag it across the text.

- Click Click on the drop-down arrow next to the font tool in the tools bar.

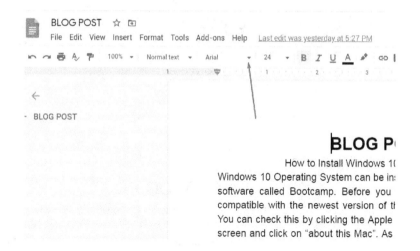

BLOG P

How to Install Windows 1(
Windows 10 Operating System can be in:
software called Bootcamp. Before you
compatible with the newest version of tl
You can check this by clicking the Apple
screen and click on "about this Mac". As

- This will show you a variety of fonts to choose from. To see more font styles, scroll down the drop-down menu using the slide bar. You either rotate the wheel on your mouse or left-click and drag the scroll bar down to reveal more font styles.

SCROLL

- If you can't find a font you like, click on "More Fonts," and it takes you to more Google fonts available. Select any font(s)

and add them to your list. Click "OK" when you are done.

Font Size

Most people set their font style and size before typing on docs, while others preferred doing that when they are done with typing.

Either way is Okay, it all depends on what you want. After choosing your font style, the next thing you need to do is set your font size. To do this, click on the drop-down arrow next to the font-size icon on the tools bar and select a particular font size.

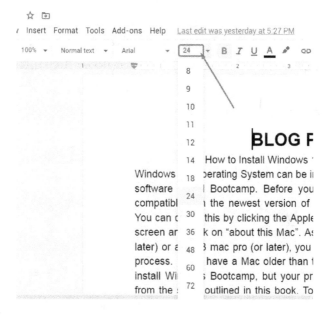

Standard Bold, Italics and Underline

B *I* <u>U</u>

Next is the standard bold, italics, and underline for text. To use any of these options, highlight the portion of the document you want boldfaced, italicized, or underlined and select either B, I or U.

Font Color

A

We can also give our text color by clicking on the text color icon. To do this, highlight the text > click on the text color icon > and pick any color from the color pane.

Text Align

The text-align tool is another crucial Docs formatting tool. It allows you to align your text to the left, center, or right. To align text within the document, highlight the texts, and click on left, center, and right alignment buttons depending on how you want the text. The last text alignment button is the justify button, which ensures texts are stretched out from the left margin to the right margin.

Line Spacing

Line spacing is a text formatting tool that determines the space between texts. You may decide to make the text on your file to have single, 1.5, or double line spacing. To do this, highlight the entire texts and click on the line spacing button on the tools menu. Select whatever spacing that suits the job.

BLOG POST

How to Install Windows 10 on MacBook Pro

ndows 10 Operating System can be installed on a MacOS wit
ftware called Bootcamp. Before you get started, ensure y
mpatible with the newest version of the Bootcamp installatio
u can check this by clicking the Apple logo in the upper-left c
een and click on "about this Mac". As long as you have a 20
er) or a 2013 mac pro (or later), you are good to go with the
cess. If you have a Mac older than those years, you will stil
tall Windows Bootcamp, but your process may look a little bit different
m the steps outlined in this book. To get started, you need a legitimate
py of Windows 10 and ISO format for this installation. This can be
rchased and downloaded directly from Microsoft website. If you choose
download from the Microsoft web page, ensure you select the April

Listing (Bullet and Number listing)

There are two types of listing on Google Docs – Number listing or Bullet listing. Either of these can be used for listing items in a document. Listing can be added to texts in several ways. The first method is to type out the list > highlight them and click on either the bullet or number listing. For instance, let's say we want to list the following items: Dog, Cat, Monkey, Rat, Lion. We will first type them out as a list as shown below.

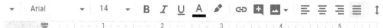

My List

Dog
Cat
Monkey
Rat
Lion

Then we highlight them.

Next, we click on the bullet list tool.

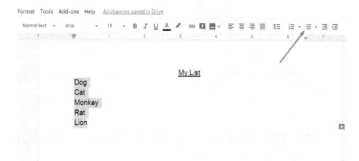

It automatically adds bullets to our list.

There are several bullet options to select from. Click on the drop-down arrow next to the bullet list icon to access them.

The same steps is used in applying numbered listing to your list.

Increase/Decrease Indent

You may wish to indent certain portions of your document, maybe a quote or a para-graph. Highlight the section the section and click on the increase indent tool ⬗.

Click on the decrease indent tool ⬗ to take it back.

Zoom

100% ▾

With the zoom tool, you can zoom-in or zoom-out your document. Click on the drop-down arrow to select between zoom percentages.

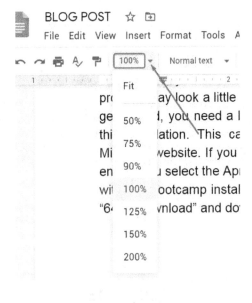

Undo/Redo

The undo function, as the name implies, will undo your last action while redo reverses the "undo" action.

Print

This action allows you to print your document if a printer is attached to your PC. You can also use the Print tool to convert your text to PDF or save it to Google Drive. To Print a document, click on the print tool on the tools bar > select the printer you wish to print from in the destination tab.

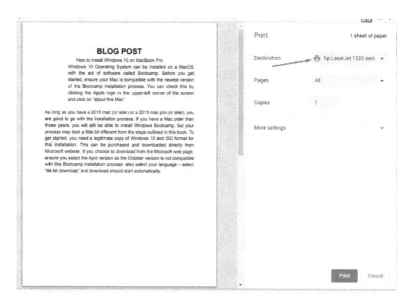

Select "All" in the pages tab if you wish to print the entire document or select "Custom" if you want to print out some pages. If

"Custom" is selected, specify the page range you want to print. Specify how many copies of the document or selected pages; you wish to print out. Finally, hit the "Print" button at the lower-right corner. If a Printer is not attached to your PC, you can convert the document to PDF and send it across. To do this, select "Save as PDF" in the Destination tab, then click "Save."

Insert Link

The "insert link" tool allows you to add a web link in your document. Highlight text > Click on the insert link icon on the toolbar > in the dialogue box that pops up, paste the web link on the "Link tab." Finally, click "Apply." This changes the text to a clickable web link.

Text

Link

Paste a link, or search   Apply

Text Styles

If you are working on a document that would require a table of content, then make use of the style function. The style feature will aid users to insert a table of content in their document automatically. When you are through typing the text, ensure the titles and subtitles you wish to have on your table of content are highlighted one after the other, and after each one is highlighted, click on the drop-down menu next to the styling tool and select Header 1. Do this for the rest of the headings.

When you are done, navigate to the page where you want your table of content to be inserted and click on "Insert" on the menu bar > click "Table of Content."

There are two ways we can insert a table of content. The first is having a text with a page number; this is a table of content with page numbers for each header. The second option is a table of content, "With Blue Links." This style is used mostly for non-print documents

(documents that will be in the digital space). It does not have page numbers but links to the pages.

You can update your table of content automatically to reflect changes to page numbers or new additions by clicking on the refresh button.

Insert Menu

There are many different things we can insert into our Google Documents using the insert menu. We will look at these items one after the other.

Inserting Image

This is the first item on the "Insert" menu. When you click on the "insert image," you will find that there are several options. The first is to upload images from your computer or device; the second option is to search the web. The advantage of using the web option for searching and inserting images is that Google filters through images with permissions for reuse. The third option is to insert an image stored on your Google drive, and the fourth option is inserting from the Google Photos app on your cloud storage. You can also use the URL option is you have a hosted image. Finally, you can insert an image from your device's webcam or any connected camera.

Tables

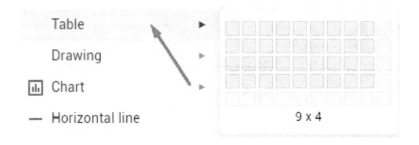

The next on the list is the "Insert Tables" option. With this option, you can select the number of rows and columns you like by simply moving your cursor across the boxes.

Drawings

There are two ways of inserting a drawing to a Google Document – You can create a drawing that is housed within Google Document, which cannot be found elsewhere except on Google document. To create this kind of drawing, click on Insert > Drawing > New. This opens a drawing platform where you can sketch whatever you wish.

Alternatively, drawings can be inserted from Google Drive by clicking on Insert > Drawing > From Drive. Then select the Google drawing file.

This way, whenever you update that single file, it will be updated in all your documents. It is excellent for schematics, overviews, or when you have students working on multiple projects but referencing a particular drawing.

Charts

With the insert chart, you can create different charts from your data set stored in Google Sheets. Here you can either insert a contained chart (just for your document) or select one from your sheets by clicking on "From Sheets."

Horizontal Lines and Footnotes

Horizontal lines and footnotes are brilient to keep things organized on our Google documents.

Headers & Footers and breaks

Headers and footers are text that appears at the top or bottom of all the pages in your document. A Header is added to a document from the "Insert" menu. To add a header to your document, click on insert > Headers & Footers > Header.

There are several header options in Google Docs. To access these features, click "options" next to the header you inserted.

The header option is how to take control of the header. You can customize your header and footer by either changing the text margins, insert different headers and footers on each page, or set odd and even pages to have different headers and footers. Having an option to customize each page requires using 'next page section breaks' to separate each page and making them stand independent of the previous page. Then, the header and footer for each page can then be customized using an extra header and footer options that will appear. You can add the custom settings to those sections alone or the entire pages on the document. This is great for printing back to front documents and for creating profess-ional-looking PDF or ebooks.

Once you have added a number of page breaks, you can then add section breaks. These different sections will allow you to have different headers or different settings for different sections in the document.

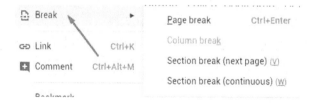

You can insert 'section breaks' by clicking on insert > Break > section break(next page).

Paint Format

If you have a document or a section of a file you have formatted, and you wish to copy the format style to another section or document, the paint format is the tool to use. Highlight the format you would like to copy over to another section and click on the paint format button, and it knows the formatting we have used. Now, whichever text, word, or paragraph or part of the text we highlight next will get that same style of formatting copied over. This is useful when you want a consistent format across your document.

Mail Collaboration

Let say you have a document, and it is shared with twenty persons (collaborators), and you only want to message two of those twenty collaborators. What you should do is click on "File" on the menu > Email collaborators.

Now, you can select the number of persons (collab-orators) you want to receive the message. Then type in your message in the message box. This gives you real control over who you are messaging.

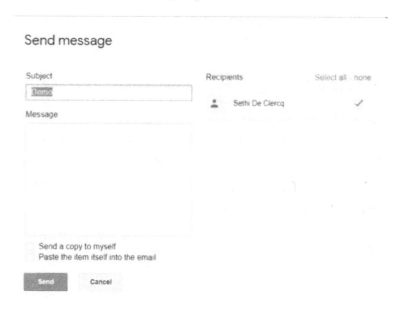

Mail As Attachment

Sometimes you may want some feedback on a document, but you don't want it to be in a collaborative setting. All you need is to mail them the document as an attachment. To do this, click on File > Email as attachment.

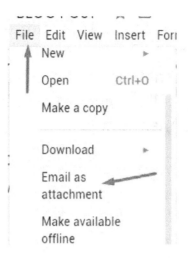

Then in the dialogue box, type in the address of the recipient(s), add a message in the message box and select what format the document should be sent.

78

Example of file type you can send the document as include –

PDF

Microsoft Word

Rich Text (RTF)

HTML

Plain Text

Open Document

Paste the item itself into the email

Downloading Document

You can download your document in several formats to your PC or device by clicking on 'File' > 'Download' > select from the several file type.

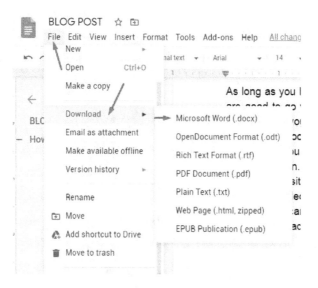

You can maintain several versions of your document to keep track of them on Google Drive. For instance, you could name your document version 1.1, 1.2, 1.3, etc. To do this, click on the file menu > version history > name current version.

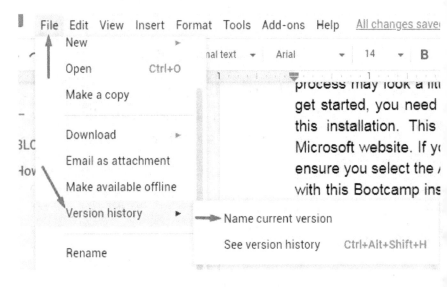

You can see all your previous version by clicking on the 'see version history.'

Page Setup

The page setup is where you choose some settings for sections of your document or the entire document. Here, you can change the margins, page background color, choose between portrait and landscape mode, select page size, etc.

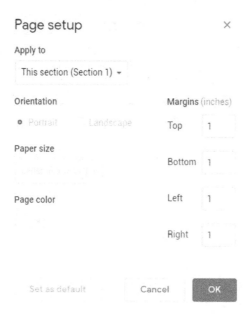

Spelling and grammar check

Advanced spelling and grammar check is one advantage typing documents on Google Docs have over Microsoft Word. It gives you a standard grammar and spelling check and also shows spelling and grammar suggestions where necessary. To carry out checks on documents, click on 'Tools' on the menu > select 'spellings and grammar' > click 'spelling and grammar check.' Next, check 'Show spelling suggestions and Show grammar suggestions' if you want the system to make suggestions for your document.

Word Count

Word count	×
Pages	3
Words	202
Characters	1140
Characters excluding spaces	945

☐ Display word count while typing

Cancel | **OK**

Word count gives a clear breakdown of every-thing about our document. It gives you the number of pages, words, and characters in your document.

We can get the active live word count to be displayed at the bottom-left of our document by checking the "Display word count while typing" in the dialogue box. This feature is ideal for checking essays, tests, examinations, articles for the word count at a glance.

Compare Document

This is a new feature of Google Docs that allows users to compare a current document with other documents already on Google Drive. This way, Google scans both documents and gives an overview of changes and who made those changes.

Compare documents ✕

Select the comparison document

☐ My Drive

Attribute differences to

Gilob Pub

☐ Include comments from the selected document

Learn more   Cancel   Compare

If you thick the "Include comments from the selected document," you will be able to see and compare collaborators' comments on the two documents under review. Once you have selected a document and clicked on the checkbox to include comments, click on the "Compare" button. This will open up a separate document where the difference and similarities between the two documents are displayed.

Explore

The explore tool is one of the powerful tools within Google docs. The 'Explore Button' can be found in the bottom-left corner of your document.

It is a web tool that combines search and other functionality. The "explore tool" is used for searching the meaning of words and images of the searched item within the document. It also does a scan of Google Drive for that keyword you are searching for.

When your search term requires you to see more on a web page, Google Doc opens up the web page on a new tab without interfering with your document. Now, if you copy any information from any of the web pages, you will be required to cite your source. To do this, hover your cursor on the website in the explore window and the "cite my source" icon pops up. Click on it to add your source as a footnote.

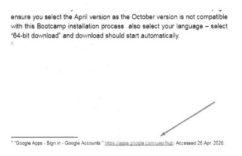

You can also change the citation format. To do that, click on the ellipses where you have "Web Results" at the top of the "explore" window.

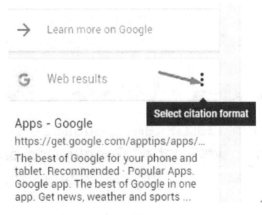

Select between MLA, APA and Chicago citation format.

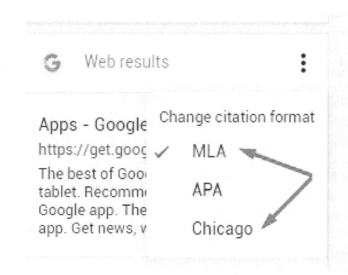

You can also insert images from the "explore" search results. Click on the image you wish to add to see a large scale version of it and click insert.

You can also insert images without previewing them by simply click, drag and drop the image into the document or clicking on the plus "+" icon that appears when you hover your cursor on an image.

Because you used the explore functionality to insert images, all the images come with additional information about their source. This feature can be turned ON or OFF.

Linked Objects

With the "Linked Object" tool, you get an overview of every single linked document within your google docs. This helps you to find similar documents saved elsewhere within Google Drive. To do this, click on tools > linked objects. This will give you an overview of every document within your google doc linked to an external file. This is handy when you have several documents on your drive.

Voice Typing

With voice typing, you are able to dictate to your Google Docs Program. This is a voice-to-text feature, which is a handy tool for people with disabilities. Voice typing can also dictate formatting and punctuation. When voice typing is activated, a microphone icon pops up on the screen. To start dictating, click on the microphone icon and speak.

The microphone icon turns red, indicating it is ready to translate your voice into text.

At this point, everything you say is translated to text on the screen.

About the Author

Derrick Richard is a tech geek with several years of experience in the ICT industry. He passionately follows latest tech trends and his passion is in figuring out the solution to complex problems.

Derrick holds a Bachelor and a Master's Degree in ICT respectively from Georgetown University, Washington DC. He lives in Sarasota, Florida.